Beyond Words: Understanding 10 Communication Missteps in Relationships

Bilal Kosovac, LMHC

Table of Contents

Introduction

It can be thrilling to encounter the person we believe is our soulmate, someone we envision spending our lives with. We may experience an unfamiliar sensation, sensing that this connection is unlike any other. Some individuals immediately know that this newfound acquaintance will be their life partner. In the initial months, perhaps even years, the relationship is marked by exhilaration; we can't fathom existence without this individual, feeling a profound sense of connection unlike any other.

But maybe that's not the case for you. You didn't feel this way; perhaps some days, you still wonder whether this person was right for you. Does this mean that your marriage is any less valid? Of course not. Does the lack of fairytale feelings mean it isn't going to last? No, of course not! Here's what it does mean: Your marriage, like all things worth keeping, will take work. That's because the idea of a "perfect" marriage, or the idea that each of us has one soulmate with whom we will never fight, with whom we will never feel like anything is wrong, is, well, *wrong!* Marriages are a lot of work. You might feel like this person was right for you from the start or look back on your relationship and see that you had to build something together. Every marriage is different. But you know what *isn't* all that different? The kind of challenges that people face when they are married.

Although you may look at your relationship and feel alone in your struggle compared to your neighbors, friends, colleagues, and others, I can guarantee you this is not the case. Don't just take my word for it – I have multiple clients who can testify. As a marriage and family therapist, I've seen it all – the highs *and* lows of marriage. Most people come to me with their lowest lows, which is why I can confidently reassure you that you aren't the only one struggling with marriage problems. After all, marriage is about compromise and agreeing to do things in a way that fits *both people* well, and that takes a lot of hard work. Not everyone is ready or willing to do so. When one person in the relationship isn't willing to meet the other person halfway, or when both people can't seem to understand where that halfway is, that's when relationship problems occur. Can you think of reasons why this is the case? I'll give you a hint: It's the key topic we will explore throughout this book.

That's right, communication! I know – communication is a bit of a buzzword right now. from online forums to television ads and even in self-help books like this one. However, it's constantly emphasized for a reason: it's crucial. Effective communication is the backbone of any healthy relationship and is pivotal in survival. When communication falters, understanding each other's needs becomes incredibly challenging, and sometimes, even discerning our desires can be elusive. While it may sound like a cliché, the truth is that communication underpins your relationship's success. I've seen one couple after the next – most of my clients! – realize that 90% of their problems could have been solved simply by clearly communicating with one another.

And there's another reason "communication" keeps coming up: People don't listen. You may realize that your communication isn't great or know it is why you are experiencing problems. Maybe you are passive-aggressive sometimes and may even notice yourself doing it, but perhaps you don't know how else to communicate. You might be worried about talking about your issues, what bothers you, what makes you annoyed or angry, because you are afraid of the other person's reaction or feel like speaking up will lead your partner to want to end your relationship. Alternatively, you might aim to evade conflict entirely, opting to agree with everything and remain silent. Paradoxically, this approach may backfire, as it could give your partner the impression that they're solely responsible for making decisions. Things don't have to stay this way. They can change, and this is what we will be looking at throughout this book.

However, I don't want to bore you with the same knowledge and tips you might have already read on *Healthline* or other self-help websites. Instead, I will give you the knowledge, examples, common mistakes people make in relationships, and what to do instead. Throughout the following few chapters, we won't just look at the theory or what big thinkers say about how we communicate. Rather, we will be looking at what you might be misunderstanding about communication in your marriage. Specifically, we will explore how communication mistakes happen, why they might happen, and how you can work on ensuring they don't happen again.

The goal is to help you see why you might have had specific problems before and, hence, help you understand what to change to make things better in the future. So, this book will touch on ten common communication mistakes you might be making and, of course, what you should be doing instead.

Let's get started!

Chapter One:
Not Listening Actively

We've all been guilty of "hearing" someone speak while we're actually plotting how to dispute or waiting for our chance to speak and prove them wrong. Hey, don't feel bad about it; we all do it, especially if we have a hard time being critiqued by others. This is, unfortunately, where I see a lot of miscommunication happening: Partners do not listen to each other. Instead, they talk at each other and then wonder why they have a hard time getting along with one another. Well, here's the answer: You don't take the time to listen to what your partner is saying, and instead, you focus on just responding without taking the time to understand where they are coming from. The solution? Active listening.

Active listening might sound like another buzzword to your ears. Again, that's because it is. We tend to make "good communication" way more complicated than it should be. At its root, communication is about sharing and receiving messages from others. In the time between sending and receiving messages, things can go wrong. We might not communicate our message clearly or misunderstand what our partner is saying. This can lead to confusion when we reply with incorrect information, making things messy and complicated. Could you relate to that yourself? Recall a moment when you and your partner engaged in a discussion, only to realize that despite initially believing you were at odds, you were actually in alignment, both "disagreeing" on the surface but "agreeing" on the fundamental points all along. And then, you laugh about the fact that all this stemmed from miscommunication. Sound about right? Well, imagine if you could avoid all the fighting and arguing and jump straight into the actual problem, or even avoid having a problem altogether because of your improved communication!

Indeed, mastering the art of active listening and effective communication can yield transformative results in your relationships. You demonstrate genuine interest and understanding by actively listening, fostering a deeper connection with your partner. This approach involves not just hearing their words but also empathizing with their emotions and perspectives. Moreover, clear and concise communication can prevent unnecessary misunderstandings and conflicts, allowing both parties to navigate challenges collaboratively and constructively. Imagine the relief of being able to address concerns openly and honestly, knowing that you and your partner are on the same page and that your words are being heard and valued. This level of communication empowers couples to build stronger bonds, resolve conflicts more effectively, and cultivate a relationship grounded in trust and mutual respect.

It *is* possible if you start listening actively. It can be hard to listen to your partner without jumping in if you feel they're not seeing things the same way you are or if their words annoy you. But you need to give it a try, and you need to make an effort to listen to what the person is saying. This is where the "active" part of listening comes in – you shouldn't just hear the sound of their voice saying words; you should try to *listen* attentively so that you understand what they're saying and where they're coming from. Then, you can respond and reflect on what they are saying. To do this, you need to start by being fully present. This entails setting aside any distractions, whether they are physical objects or mental preoccupations, and directing your complete attention to the individual before you and their words. *Really listen.* Be present with all your senses: Make eye contact, shift your body toward them, and show that you are actually actively listening. It's essential to silence your inner dialogue that impulse or voice constantly reacting to what your partner is saying. Give it a temporary break. Allowing it to persist undermines your ability to genuinely listen to your partner.

Secondly, attuning to your partner's non-verbal signals is crucial. Studies indicate that a significant portion of communication, upwards of 65%, occurs through non-verbal cues. Therefore, paying attention to your partner's body language can provide valuable insights into their emotions and comfort level during conversations. For instance, observing their speaking pace can indicate whether they feel at ease or uneasy. Adjusting your approach accordingly, such as offering reassurance if they appear tense, can enhance the quality of your interaction. Monitoring your non-verbal cues is equally essential. Are you displaying openness through relaxed body language or inadvertently conveying defensiveness by crossing your arms or rolling your eyes? Your non-verbal behavior communicates volumes, often speaking louder than words, and can significantly impact the dynamics of your conversation. Thus, being mindful of both your partner's and your non-verbal cues fosters a more profound understanding and connection in your relationship.

Next up, try to ask some open-ended questions. You may have encountered discussions where someone asked, "Do you agree that ___?" and even if you did in principle, they didn't allow you the opportunity to express your own feelings. Instead, you had to fit within that binary box – yes or no. Instead of boxing your partner in, ask questions that give them enough space to share their thoughts and feelings. Instead of asking a yes or no question, ask them to tell you more about what they are sharing with you. Ask them what they're thinking about, what they believe is the best way to move forward, and so on. Don't take away their ability to tell you how they think and feel. It would be best if you had an open and productive conversation with one another.

In addition to active listening, it's vital to demonstrate understanding and validation during conversations with your partner. This involves affirming their thoughts and feelings by accurately summarizing what they've expressed. After your partner has finished speaking, please take a moment to reflect on what they've said and then paraphrase it back to them. This shows that you were actively listening and allows you to confirm your understanding of their perspective. Ask them if your interpretation aligns with their intended meaning or if there are any points you may need to understand better. By seeking clarification this way, you ensure that your response is grounded in an accurate understanding of their thoughts and emotions.

Furthermore, validating your partner's feelings validates their experiences, promoting empathy and mutual respect. When you acknowledge and validate your partner's emotions, you create a safe space for them to express themselves openly and honestly. This validation doesn't necessarily mean agreeing with everything they say but instead acknowledging the validity of their feelings and perspectives. This validation fosters trust and understanding, strengthening the emotional connection between you and your partner.

Finally, maintaining patience and refraining from passing judgment are crucial components of effective communication in any relationship. It can be challenging, especially when you strongly believe in your perspective and feel your partner may need to grasp the situation or share your viewpoint fully. Creating space for your partner to express their thoughts and feelings can be particularly challenging when you feel entrenched in your perspective. However, it's essential to prioritize active listening and empathy, especially within the marriage or any significant relationship. A genuine desire to understand your partner's perspective and ensure they feel heard is paramount. They shouldn't feel rushed or pressured to articulate their thoughts before you interject with expressing your opinion; refraining from passing judgment is essential.

When your partner opens up about how your actions affected them or shared their emotions, the last thing they need is to feel criticized or condemned by you. Instead, approach these conversations with an open mind and heart, seeking to understand and support your partner without judgment or criticism. This approach fosters trust, respect, and emotional intimacy, ultimately strengthening the bond between you and your partner.

Overall, it's necessary to recognize that disagreements and differing perspectives are natural aspects of any relationship. Even if your partner expresses views that you don't agree with or perceive as inaccurate, it's essential to give them the space to voice their thoughts and feelings. Listening attentively, validating their perspective, and responding empathetically is critical to fostering a healthy and respectful dialogue. It's crucial to show that you value and respect your partner enough to engage with their viewpoint, even if it differs from yours.

By remaining empathetic and demonstrating genuine care for their feelings and perspective, you affirm the strength of your bond and reinforce mutual trust and understanding in the relationship. Remember, effective communication isn't about winning arguments or proving oneself right; it's about building a deeper connection and fostering mutual respect and appreciation for each other's perspectives.

Desire Dialogue for Couples: Using Active Listening

Objective: Explore wants and needs to strengthen your connection using assertive and active listening skills. Take a minute to think about what could be improved in the relationship.

Identify Desires:

Each of you will list three desires for the relationship.

Examples:

- More spontaneous adventures.
- Less unresolved conflicts.
- More expressions of appreciation.

Exchange:

Share your lists while practicing assertiveness and active listening.

> Speaker's Turn:
> - Express desires using "I" statements (e.g., "I wish...").
> - Describe how life improves when wishes come true.
>
>> E.g., "I wish for more spontaneous adventures—it adds excitement and lasting memories."

> Listener's Role:
> - Recap to confirm understanding.
> - Illuminate the wish and its emotional impact. Example: "You would like us to add excitement and make lasting memories by being more spontaneous. Is that right?"

Post-Dialogue:

Reflect on:

Assertiveness:

- How well did you express desires?
- What challenges did you encounter in voicing wishes?

Active Listening:

- In what instances did active listening deepen understanding?
- Discuss these moments and their impact.

This tool can be beneficial as it encourages partners to openly communicate their desires, fostering a deeper understanding of each other's needs. By promoting assertiveness and active listening, this exercise contributes to building stronger connections and addressing any challenges in the relationship.

Reflection Questions:

As you reflect on the lists outlining your desires, do you notice any recurring themes or patterns that seem to connect your individual wants and needs within the context of the relationship?

_____

_____

_____

Did sharing your desires lead to new insights or discoveries about each other's aspirations for the relationship?

_____

_____

_____

Reflecting on your role as the speaker, how effectively were you able to express your desires using "I" statements?

_____

_____

_____

Were there any desires you found particularly challenging to articulate? If so, what made them difficult to voice?

_____

_____

_____

As the listener, how successfully did you accurately summarize and understand your partner's desires?

_____

_____

_____

Did any of your partner's wishes surprise you or offer a new perspective on their needs within the relationship?

_____

_____

_____

Discuss any challenges or obstacles you encountered during the dialogue process. How did you navigate these challenges together?

_____

_____

_____

In what ways did engaging in this exercise foster growth and understanding between you as a couple?

_____

_____

_____

Can you recall moments during the exchange where active listening deepened your understanding of your partner's desires?

_____

_____

_____

How did these moments of enhanced understanding contribute to strengthening your connection or resolving potential misunderstandings?

_____

_____

_____

How do you envision integrating the skills and insights gained from this exercise into your daily interactions and communication within the relationship?

_____

_____

_____

Are there any specific strategies or practices you plan to implement to ensure ongoing open dialogue and mutual understanding regarding your desires and needs?

_____

_____

_____

Chapter Two: Avoiding Difficult Conversations

In the course of our lives, we engage in a myriad of conversations, ranging from mundane daily discussions to more meaningful exchanges. Regarding our relationships, these conversations with our partners encompass various topics and decisions that shape our shared lives. From practical matters such as meal planning and holiday arrangements to more profound discussions about finances, future goals, and personal preferences, these conversations are essential for maintaining harmony and understanding in the relationship.

However, the actual test of communication skills arises when we encounter complex or uncomfortable topics. These crucial discussions often revolve around sensitive issues such as finances, intimacy, and personal values. Despite their importance, potential conflict, or misunderstanding, we may encounter these subjects and inadvertently avoid addressing critical topics, leading to unresolved tensions and challenges within the relationship.

For example, discussions about financial planning and budgeting can be particularly daunting, especially if partners have differing attitudes or priorities regarding money management. Similarly, conversations about intimacy and emotional needs require vulnerability and openness, which can be challenging for some individuals to navigate.

Furthermore, cultural and societal norms may influence our willingness to engage in certain discussions, specific hesitancy, or discomfort in addressing topics that are deemed taboo; avoiding these conversations can hinder the growth and development of the relationship, allowing partners to truly understand needs.

Ultimately, effective communication fosters trust, intimacy, and mutual respect in a relationship. By acknowledging the importance of difficult conversations and embracing them as opportunities for growth and understanding, you can strengthen your bond and navigate challenges with greater ease and resilience.

Now, there is more to this. Without going full therapist mode on you, I want to explore a few concepts. In relationships, there are different attachment styles. These attachment styles determine many things, from how we show love to how we feel when our relationships are not entirely secure. Attachment styles are essential when we think about conflict. Conflict happens in all relationships and to different degrees. But when someone finds conflict extremely scary, difficult conversations might be avoided.

In relationships, attachment styles are the patterns of behavior and emotional responses that individuals develop based on their early interactions with caregivers. These styles significantly influence how individuals perceive and engage in intimate relationships. There are four primary attachment styles: secure, anxious-preoccupied, dismissive-avoidant, and fearful-avoidant.

Individuals with a secure attachment style feel at ease with intimacy and trust in relationships. They are adept at communicating their emotions openly and have a positive self-image and outlook on their partners. Conversely, individuals with an anxious-preoccupied attachment style crave intimacy and approval but often struggle with anxiety and fear of rejection. They may be hypersensitive to signs of abandonment and require reassurance from their partners.

In contrast, those with a dismissive-avoidant attachment style prioritize independence and self-sufficiency. They may downplay the importance of close relationships and find it challenging to express vulnerability or rely on others for support. Fearful-avoidant attachment, also known as disorganized attachment, combines elements of anxious-preoccupied and dismissive-avoidant styles. Individuals with this style desire intimacy but fear rejection and may have difficulty trusting others.

Understanding these attachment styles offers valuable insights into how you and your partner might navigate conflict and communication within relationships. For instance, those with a secure attachment style may approach conflicts constructively, whereas individuals with anxious-preoccupied or dismissive-avoidant styles may struggle with communication and avoidance of difficult conversations.

Navigating tough conversations presents unique hurdles influenced by individuals' attachment styles. Anxious attachment styles, rooted in a fear of abandonment, may amplify the challenges of such discussions. These individuals often fear that confronting issues could destabilize the relationship, heightening anxiety about potential breakup scenarios. Conversely, those with avoidant attachment styles, emphasizing independence and emotional distance, may resist opening up and revealing vulnerability under challenging conversations.

While anxious individuals grapple with the fear of disconnection, avoidant individuals wrestle with acknowledging and confronting their emotions. Consequently, these differing attachment styles contribute to the complexities of engaging in challenging discussions, presenting distinct obstacles for individuals seeking effective communication and resolution within their relationships.

Consider how you typically approach difficult conversations. Are you adept at expressing your emotions and addressing tough topics head-on, or are you shying away from such discussions? You may view these conversations as integral to everyday communication, recognizing the need for additional empathy and consideration when broaching sensitive subjects. On the other hand, do you perceive these discussions as battlegrounds, where the objective is to emerge victorious at the expense of your partner's feelings? Reflecting on your communication style can provide valuable insights into your conflict resolution and relationship dynamics approach. Cultivating open and honest communication lays the foundation for a healthier, more fulfilling partnership.

The answer to those questions can reveal why you avoid the big questions as long as possible.

You might shy away from these discussions because maintaining stability seems safer than risking disruption. However, avoiding them prevents you from preparing for the inevitable challenges ahead. When these issues eventually arise, you can't ignore them. For instance, if you've avoided discussing scenarios like a parent falling ill and needing to relocate for their care or one of you securing a job in another city, it may temporarily reassure you that everything will remain okay. However, when these situations materialize, it can feel like your world is unraveling because you haven't addressed them beforehand.

There's more to difficult conversations. Sometimes, only one of you needs to talk about something on your mind, and the thought of talking about the subject is highly nerve-wracking. To return to attachment styles, this may be because you are afraid of opening up, or maybe you are worried that any conversation that isn't rainbows and unicorns is going to lead to a breakup. But this isn't accurate. This is anxiety or fear talking, not reality. The dialogue must happen because silence only leads to unresolved issues and resentment. If you both avoid talking about things that upset you or if you both avoid talking about the "real issues" because you are worried about the potential outcome, you are both setting yourselves up for years of anger, frustration, and, ultimately, for therapy to make things work out again!

So, it would be best if you had the difficult conversations. You need to face your fears. Perhaps that means that you both personally need to go to therapy to figure out why you are struggling to talk about your emotions or something that frustrates you so you can learn how to cope with that anxiety. Regardless of what it may be, you cannot avoid having challenging discussions. They will come back and bite you.

These conversations do not need to be extremely difficult, and they don't have to be anxiety-inducing. You can mitigate how stressful they are by simply speaking to your partner about your stress and sharing that you are worried about the conversation's outcome. This person loves you and cares for you, so sharing this with them will most likely make them a lot more empathetic and help them ensure they are ready to be responsive, attentive, and kind to you – even more than usual.

Consider how your communication may have been a struggle lately, partly because of your obstacles in discussing less enjoyable topics. Can you think of a conversation that you know you should be having but are avoiding because of the potential outcome or because it just makes things uncomfortable? If so, it may be why you feel like you need to be more connected. It might also be the reason why you might end up building resentment towards one another. You need to talk, and you need to do so openly and honestly. Share your feelings, fears, and worries, and avoid being as nervous about the outcome. Think about the potential good things that could come out of this exchange.

If you think it'll help, plan to get therapy for yourself to explore why you may not like going through the difficult discussions. Many of us dislike them. After all, avoiding problems and seeking peace is human nature. But if you actively avoid them, and if avoiding these uncomfortable conversations often leads you to be in a position where you put everyone else, including your partner, before yourself (i.e., people-pleasing), or if you feel like you can never fully express yourself or your concerns. You prefer to be quiet rather than potentially disagree with your partner; you need to figure out why.

A quick and final note – if you are scared of speaking up and having difficult conversations with your partner due to their temper or because they are abusive or violent, do not just seek therapy: Seek help so you can exit this situation.

Navigating Difficult Conversations Exercise for Couples: Building Constructive Dialogue

Objective: Enhance communication skills and foster both partner's ability to have a constructive dialogue while navigating difficult conversations.

Materials Needed:

- Timer (optional)
- Comfortable and quiet space for discussion

Steps:

Choose a Difficult Topic:

Select a challenging topic related to emotions, conflicts, or future plans that needs discussion.

Set Ground Rules:

Establish clear ground rules for a respectful conversation.

- Use "I" statements.
- Avoid blame or accusations.
- No interrupting. Allow each person to express themselves fully.
- Take turns speaking and listening.

Speaker-Listener Rotation:

Decide a set time limit for each person to be the speaker initially (e.g., five minutes).

- The speaker shares thoughts, feelings, and perspectives on the chosen topics.
- The listener actively listens without interrupting until the speaker finishes.

Reflective Response:

After the speaker finishes, the listener reflects on what they hear, adding opinions.

- Ensure the speaker feels understood and provides an opportunity for clarification.

Open Dialogue and Reflection:

Engage in an open dialogue using insights gained to discuss potential solutions, compromises, or ways to move forward.

- Reflect on the experience together, discussing what worked well and areas for improvement.

Reflection Questions:

How did you both feel about engaging in this exercise together?

_____

_____

_____

Did the structured format help facilitate a more productive conversation compared to your usual discussions?

_____

_____

_____

Reflecting on the chosen topic, were there any unexpected insights or revelations that arose during the conversation?

_____

_____

_____

Did discussing this particular topic deepen your understanding of each other's perspectives or emotions?

_____

_____

_____

Were you able to maintain the established ground rules throughout the exercise? If not, what challenges did you encounter?

_____

_____

_____

Which ground rule(s) do you feel were the most beneficial in promoting effective communication?

_____

_____

_____

How did you perceive the balance of being heard and understood when taking on the roles of both the speaker and the listener?

_____

_____

_____

As the listener, how did it feel to reflect back on the speaker's thoughts and feelings? Did you find it challenging or enlightening?

_____

_____

_____

As the speaker, how would you describe the extent to which your partner's reflective responses, did they accurately capture your perspective?

_____

_____

_____

What key insights or solutions emerged from the open dialogue phase of the exercise?

_____

_____

_____

Are there specific compromises or action steps you both agreed upon to address the discussed topic moving forward?

_____

_____

_____

How do you envision incorporating the skills and strategies learned from this exercise into your future conversations?

_____

_____

_____

Are there any adjustments or improvements you would like to make to enhance the effectiveness of similar exercises in the future?

_____

_____

_____

Chapter Three:
Using Absolute Language

Have you ever experienced that moment of irritation when you blurt out, "This always happens," or "You always do this"? It's a common reaction, often brushed off as insignificant. But here's the thing: those seemingly harmless remarks can pack a punch, setting off a chain reaction with severe implications for your relationship. Using a word like *always* or *never* can be exceedingly hurtful and destroy your marriage. If your partner feels like they're *never* right like they are always in the wrong, or like you are always about to nag them about something new… Then, of course, they'll feel like they are doing everything they can not to annoy you. Look at it the other way around – how would you feel if someone told you "You never…" or "You always…" in a negative context? Of course, there comes a moment when repeating the same thing becomes annoying, but this doesn't excuse using absolute language. Does your partner really *never* do that one thing? Do they really *always* act this way? Or are you just annoyed at this moment, and you are now taking it out on them for no specific reason?

Using this language will likely have the opposite effect you intend – it's likely to make your partner quite defensive. After all, you *are* accusing them of never, or always, doing something specific. So, it feels right to counter-argue by saying they aren't correct and to point out the times when you did or *didn't* do that. It's only normal – you want to show them their statement is wrong.

But does that genuinely help communication? Does that help you both come to an agreement, share a perspective, and come to a common ground? Or does it only pit you against one another and lead to a conversation that is anything but productive? I place my bets on the latter.

Now, what can you do to avoid this? Well, start by considering the alternatives. You might feel it's true that they "never" do this or that they "always" do this, but even if it's true, it won't lead to the kind of outcome that you are after. Instead, you need to consider the type of conversation and communication that will lead to a positive outcome. So, consider how else you can express your message.

How can you communicate how you feel without making them feel like they are always in the wrong? Think about times when they did or did not do that very thing – can you think of any? Try to remember exceptions. If not, try to think about how you can communicate this. Could you, for example, tell them that you dislike the current state of things? For example, if you are annoyed because they "never" take out the trash, could you, instead, say, "I feel like I am the one who takes out the trash the most between us two, and I would like to see that task become more equally split?"

This is an excellent way to share how you feel about the event, instead of instantly telling them that they are doing something wrong, that you are unhappy with how they act, and, therefore, with *them* specifically. In other words, you should separate the action from the person so your partner can feel less defensive.

While it's common to inadvertently use sweeping statements in the heat of the moment, being mindful of this language can significantly impact the quality of your communication. If you catch yourself using absolute terms, consider acknowledging it by saying, "I realize that my choice of words might not capture the full picture, but it seems like there's a pattern of this behavior." This acknowledgment opens the door for a more constructive discussion with your partner, allowing both of you to collaboratively address the issue, reshape the dynamic, and work together to prevent it from becoming a recurring challenge in your relationship.

In the big picture, avoiding absolutes is crucial because they can create an atmosphere of blame and defensiveness. Recognize that, despite recurring issues, expressing them without using sweeping language allows for a more open and understanding discussion. After all, relationships thrive when there's a willingness to talk about concerns without laying blame on each other.

Positive Connection Exercise for Couples: Nurturing Joyful Moments

Objective: Enhance positive communication and deepen connection within the relationship.

Process:

Spontaneous Gratitude Sharing:

> Embrace moments of spontaneous gratitude. Whenever you feel a surge of appreciation or joy, express it to your partner. This can be as simple as acknowledging their presence, sharing a laugh, or expressing gratitude for a small gesture. No formal journaling is required.
>
> **Psychoeducation:** This practice fosters a continuous flow of positive energy, promoting an atmosphere of appreciation and gratitude in your relationship.

Heartfelt Compliment Moments:

> Make a conscious effort to spontaneously compliment your partner when you notice something you genuinely appreciate. It could be their kindness, sense of humor, or a specific action. Allow compliments to arise naturally in the course of your interactions.

Psychoeducation: Genuine compliments boost self-esteem and reinforce positive behaviors, contributing to a more positive relationship dynamic.

Reflective Affirmation Exchange:

During moments of reflection or quiet time together, share affirmations naturally. Speak from the heart about the qualities you admire in each other. These affirmations can occur in casual conversations rather than a structured session.

Psychoeducation: Affirmations contribute to a sense of security and emotional well-being in a relationship, fostering a positive emotional environment.

Mindful Appreciation Conversations:

Engage in organic conversations about what you appreciate in each other. This can happen during a quiet evening, a walk, or a shared activity. Discuss specific behaviors, qualities, or experiences that positively affect the relationship.

Psychoeducation: Mindful appreciation conversations deepen emotional connection and create shared positive memories, contributing to relationship satisfaction.

Reflection Questions:

Did you find expressing spontaneous gratitude towards your partner challenging or rewarding? Why or why not?

_____

_____

_____

Can you recall specific moments when expressing gratitude enhanced your connection or brought you closer?

_____

_____

_____

Reflecting on the compliments exchanged, how did it feel to receive genuine appreciation from your partner?

_____

_____

_____

Did you notice any changes in your partner's demeanor or mood when receiving compliments? How did it impact your relationship dynamic?

_____

_____

_____

Share the experience of exchanging affirmations with your partner. Did it deepen your appreciation for each other's qualities?

_____

_____

_____

How did receiving affirmations from your partner make you feel? Did it reinforce positive aspects of your self-image or relationship?

_____

_____

_____

Discuss any memorable conversations you had about appreciating each other's qualities or actions. What made these conversations meaningful?

_____

_____

_____

In what ways did engaging in mindful appreciation conversations contribute to a sense of emotional connection and shared positive memories?

_____

_____

_____

Moving forward, how do you plan to continue fostering moments of positivity and connection within your relationship?

_____

_____

_____

Are there any specific practices or habits you would like to incorporate to sustain a culture of gratitude, compliments, affirmations, and mindful appreciation in your daily interactions?

_____

_____

_____

Chapter Four:
Non-Verbal Communication

We've already briefly discussed this earlier, but let's consider it in more detail. Whenever you talk to your partner, you cannot focus only on the "what." You also have to consider the "how" in your communication. In other words, the bulk of your message comes from how you say things, not just the message itself. For example, you might be trying to tell your partner that you are tired of having to do the bulk of the housework alone, but if you say it by making fun of them, belittling the fact that they work long hours, or by rolling your eyes whenever they share their views, you aren't sending the message that you are genuinely open to having this conversation.

There are nine kinds of nonverbal communication types. For example, facial expressions convey how we feel, what we think, and whether we agree with whatever someone is saying. We all know these well – we smile when we are happy, cry when we are sad, roll our eyes when we disagree with something or someone, and so on. Our facial expressions are powerful communication tools because they manage to say what words sometimes can't. However, they can also be used in the wrong way. In fact, they can be manipulative. If we are talking to our partner in a way that appears open while using our facial expressions to convey a different message (for example, looking annoyed or angry but saying in a passive-aggressive manner, "Yes, I'm open to talking" followed by an eye roll), we are sending mixed messages.

It would also benefit your relationship and how you communicate to be mindful of your gestures. The way you use your hands, arms, and legs speaks volumes. Engaging in vigorous waving or abrupt arm movements sends a clear message – you're not open to discussion; instead, you're visibly upset. This doesn't create a conducive environment for productive conversation or make your partner feel at ease. Instead, maintaining a calm, relaxed posture with your limbs can foster more positive interaction. Use your hands to illustrate points or to convey reassurance and connection to your partner.

Thirdly, consider the paralinguistic aspect of communication – encompassing the tone and volume of your voice. While passion is a natural aspect of being human, expressing intense emotions by raising your voice or adopting an aggressive tone does not encourage effective communication with your partner. Engaging in conversation with your significant other requires a kind, inviting, warm, and empathetic tone. Creating an atmosphere where they feel safe sharing their thoughts is essential. Using a harsh tone or speaking loudly can have the opposite effect. Therefore, it's crucial to keep your voice calm. If you find yourself getting louder, reflect on why that might happen and silently remind yourself of the person you're addressing – your spouse or partner, deserving of your utmost care and kindness. After all, shouldn't they expect the best version of you, just as you do from them?

Fourth, pay attention to your body language. Oftentimes, this is what betrays us! We might try to appear open to the conversation, but our crossed legs and arms say the opposite. If your body language is relatively closed, consider why that's the case. Then, relax your body. Remember – communication is necessary for all partnerships, and yours is no different. So, open yourself up and think about how you can approach this conversation from a more positive and open perspective and how you can demonstrate this physically.

Fifth, we speak with our personal space. When you are annoyed at your partner, you might not want to hold their hand. You might want to shift your body away from them. You might not want them anywhere close to you. You might just want them to give you some space. Well, that is also communication! You are sending your partner a message by protecting your personal space and limiting the amount of space they can take from you. This shows them how you feel about them at that moment. So, be careful not to hurt their feelings by only using body language. Instead of swatting their hand away, you can use your words to explain that you need space. You can tell them that you don't feel like kissing or hugging at that moment because you need a bit of space but that you'll be ready to connect with them later. These are all things that can be communicated! This is also close to haptics, or *touch*, which is another way in which we communicate (the sixth way).

Seventh, there is eye contact. Sometimes, when we are annoyed with someone, we don't want to look at them. However, this can be exceedingly hurtful to your partner because it can make them feel like you are shutting them out. Instead, remember that this is your partner and that this is a conversation. Show them the respect you would like to be shown. You don't need to jump into their arms and accept their apology or say that everything is fine, but do look at them when they are speaking, and vice versa.

Now, circling back to the last two nonverbal communication types—your appearance and artifacts. While these aspects play a role in communication, we'll park them on the sidelines for now since they may not be as immediately relevant to our ongoing discussions.

In summary, every time you engage in a conversation with your partner, it's crucial to extend your focus beyond the words you're vocalizing. Consider the potential impact your nonverbal cues might be wielding during the exchange.

Before you dive into the next dialogue, pause for a moment of reflection. Recollect any feedback you've received in past conversations. Perhaps your partner has mentioned that eye-rolling doesn't sit well with them. Alternatively, think back to interactions with your parents—did they ever point out defensive behaviors, tone issues, or attitude concerns? Unfortunately, many of us tend to carry over less-than-ideal communication styles into our relationships, resulting in unproductive and sometimes hurtful conversations.

Let's break this cycle and actively work on cultivating nonverbal communication that fosters an environment for partners to share their genuine feelings and thoughts openly. Steering away from counterproductive habits can pave the way for more constructive and enriching conversations.

Body Language Awareness Exercise for Couples: Enhancing Non-Verbal Communication

Objective: Increase awareness of body language and its impact on communication within the relationship.

Setting Intentions:

> Start by discussing the purpose of the exercise with your partner. Share the goal of enhancing communication by becoming more aware of body language cues.

Conscious Observation:

> Throughout the day, consciously observe your body language in various situations. Pay close attention to your facial expressions, posture, and gestures.
> Take note of how your non-verbal cues may influence your communication dynamics.

Adjustments and Reflection:

> Make intentional adjustments to your body language to align with the message.
> For instance, be mindful of maintaining the language during discussions on sensitive topics.
> Reflect on any insights gained from being conscious of your body language and how it impacts your interactions.

Partner Observation:

> Encourage your partner to engage in the same exercise, focusing on their own body language throughout the day.
>
> Share observations and reflections with each other to foster open communication and understanding.

Joint Reflection and Action Plan:

> Come together as a couple to discuss your experiences.
>
> Share insights about the role of body language in your communication and how it has affected your interactions.
>
> Identify specific actions or adjustments you can both make to enhance discussions in the future.

Reflection Questions:

How did discussing the purpose of the exercise with your partner enhance your understanding of the importance of body language in communication?

_____

_____

_____

Did setting intentions help you approach the exercise with a specific focus? If so, how did it impact your observations?

_____

_____

_____

Reflect on your experience of consciously observing your body language throughout the day. What key observations did you make about your facial expressions, posture, and gestures in different situations?

_____

_____

_____

Did you notice any patterns or tendencies in your non-verbal cues that you were previously unaware of?

_____

_____

_____

Describe any intentional adjustments you made to your body language during conversations or interactions. How did these adjustments affect the overall communication dynamics?

_____

_____

_____

What insights did you gain from reflecting on the impact of your body language on communication? How do you plan to apply these insights in future interactions?

_____

_____

_____

Share about your partner's engagement in the exercise. Did they also observe their own body language? How did their observations compare to yours?

_____

_____

_____

Discuss any observations or insights you gained from observing your partner's body language. Did it provide new perspectives on their communication style?

_____

_____

_____

During the joint reflection, what did you discover about the role of body language in your communication as a couple?

_____

_____

_____

Identify specific actions or adjustments both partners can make to enhance non-verbal communication in future interactions. How do you envision implementing these changes to improve communication dynamics?

_____

_____

_____

Chapter Five:
Bringing Up the Past

Let's imagine that you are currently going through a conflict with your partner because you disagree about moving to a different state for their work because of the impact this could have on your children and your life – having to move schools, find new friends, buy a new home, and the list goes on. During this conflict, the conversation initially remains on the pros and the cons. It might be a big move, but it would also give you a sizable salary increase, which would help you as a family. You could afford to pay for a private school for the kids, you could travel together more often, and you wouldn't have to work such long hours. Your partner, however, feels like this isn't suitable for the kids. It's too big a move; they're in the middle of their childhood, so they need consistency and stability, and it would be a logistical nightmare.

But then, the conversation takes a turn when you say, "You always do this – there's something exciting happening, and instead of being happy and wanting to make it work out, you find a way to make it look like a terrible idea… This is just like what happened in Florida." Suddenly, your partner tells you, "What does this have to do with Florida?!" and there you go – you've started a conflict in what was meant to be a simple conversation. What could have been a calm and composed discussion is now an argument in which your partner feels they have to fight you and protect themselves from your accusation (remember– no "always!"), and likewise feels like they're being brought back in time. Bonus points because you never actually told them that you were upset back then, so now they feel like they have been lied to.

This is what happens when you bring the past into the conversation as an argument. If you are rehashing old disagreements or issues to support your opinion, you are only escalating the conflict. You aren't thinking about the present conflict; you are only focused on being "right" in this situation and are resorting to petty (yes, it is petty!) means to get your point across. What happened in the past should stay in the past – it isn't needed in this conversation. To continue with our example, this conversation is about whether your family should move to a different state, not about whether you feel supported or ns is a conversation you can have with each other at a different time, but if you currently have an essential conversation to get through, this is not the time to turn to past events to try and make a point.

However, there are moments when bringing up the past is acceptable. For example, if you are having a conflict about something that you have discussed often with your partner, they continue to forget or willingly avoid even thinking about what you are telling them. You rely on the right to tell them that this isn't the first time you have told them about this and that you'd like to discuss it to see why this isn't changing. For example, if this had been a conversation about leaving the toilet seat up, and if you had once again walked into the bathroom and seen the toilet seat up although you had asked him to stop leaving it up for two years now, then of course, it makes sense to bring up the past! The bottom line is that it shouldn't be brought up if it isn't relevant to the current issue being discussed.

If you are tempted to bring up the past, try to think about what your rationale is. Why do you feel like this is a good tactic? Why do you want to shift the focus of the conversation to something that isn't related to the real problem at hand? Do you feel there are underlying issues that aren't being discussed, and this is an excellent opportunity for you to put these back on the table? If this is the case, I still encourage you to pause the conversation and take a moment to yourself before the past. Take some time to think about your needs and whether you need to have this conversation later on with your partner. But don't make your partner feel responsible for not knowing that they did something wrong in the past, and don't make them feel like they are being accused of something. It is a conversation killer, and it makes what *could* be a productive conversion one that is difficult to have successfully.

Nostalgic Connection Exercise for Couples: Rekindling Love Through Memories

Objective: Strengthen emotional connection by revisiting and cherishing old memories together.

Gather Sentimental Items:

Take some time to collect items associated with cherished memories in your relationship. These can include photo albums, letters, cards, or gifts that hold sentimental value.

Create a Nostalgic Space:

Find a comfortable and quiet space to go through these items together. Create an atmosphere conducive to reflection and shared sentimentality.

Share Stories and Recollections:

As you go through each item, take turns sharing recollections associated with those memories. Relive the moments and discuss how they made you feel. Allow the conversation to flow naturally.

Express Gratitude:

Express gratitude for the positive experiences and gestures you've shared in the past. Acknowledge the kindness and love expressed in those moments. Take a moment to appreciate each other for the role you played in your roles.

Affectionate Reflection:

Conclude the exercise by reflecting on how revisiting these memories has impacted your current connection. Share any newfound insights or emotions that have arisen. End the session with a gesture of affection, whether a hug, a kiss, or a simple expression of love.

Reflection Questions:

Describe the process of collecting items associated with cherished memories in your relationship. Did it evoke any emotions or anticipation for the exercise?

_____

_____

_____

Reflect on the atmosphere you created for revisiting old memories together. How did the environment contribute to the overall experience?

_____

_____

_____

Share the memories you revisited during the exercise. Which moments stood out to you the most, and why?

_____

_____

_____

How did sharing recollections and reliving those moments together impact your emotional connection?

_____

_____

_____

Discuss the expressions of gratitude exchanged during the exercise. How did acknowledging past kindness and love deepen your appreciation for each other?

_____

_____

_____

Did expressing gratitude evoke any new feelings or insights about your relationship?

_____

_____

_____

Reflect on the overall impact of revisiting old memories on your current connection. How did it contribute to a renewed sense of appreciation and love?

_____

_____

_____

Share any newfound insights or emotions that arose during the exercise. How do you plan to carry these feelings forward in your relationship?

_____

_____

_____

Chapter Six:
Failing to Compromise

When we get into our first relationships, we are often told that relationships are all about compromise. Perhaps we don't quite realize it at first because our relationships are young, innocent, and full of puppy love. But as we grow up, our priorities change, and so do the what and who we are in relationships (i.e., the role we play). The questions and decisions involved are entirely different. It's no longer "Do you want to go to prom with me?" but rather, "Are we going to move to a different state?" (I promise, I'll stop using that example now!) Relationships are a union of two people (or more, sometimes). You effectively join your life with your partner and become a *union*. This doesn't mean that you lose your individuality. It does, however, mean that you need to make some compromises here and there. You are two different people, so disagreement, different perspectives, and other values are all part of a relationship.

When it comes to communication, this idea is necessary. You aren't. You aren't hoping to reach a compromise. Instead, you are only going in with one goal – to be right and get what you want. Well, if your partner does the same thing, what do you think will happen? Will you end up productively speaking to each other, so you both agree on *a few things* but accept that as a compromise? It is improbable. Instead, you are much more likely to end up in a conflict with no end in sight because neither one of you is willing to take a step back and accept that you cannot get all you want.

In all seriousness, if you want to communicate your perspective and feel heard, you must be willing to do the same for your partner. Don't see a conversation as a battleground. See it as a way to openly discuss with your partner and share your views and perspectives with them. See it as a way to agree with one another and for you two to feel connected and on the same page. The compromise has to be mutual, not one-sided.

But besides this, you need to come into the conversation with good intent. You should be willing to speak to your partner about an issue and to come from a "good place" with them. In other words, you want to be coming from a place that is empathetic and kind, not from a place that is focused on only getting what you want or trying to convince your partner to give you what you want even if you know that it's nowhere near what *they* want. This can even be manipulative! Suppose you try to come to a "compromise" while primarily expecting to get what you want and rely on your partner's feelings to make them willing to give you what you want. In that case, you must consider whether you are approaching the discussion healthily.

You should both want what's best for each other, even if it's not 100% what *you* want individually.

Compromise and Collaboration Exercise for Couples: Strengthening Partnership

Objective: Develop the skill of finding win-win solutions through compromise and collaboration to strengthen your relationship.

Choosing a Scenario

Select a non-sensitive scenario or topic that requires decision-making, such as planning a weekend activity or dividing household responsibilities.

Independent Brainstorming

Individually, brainstorm different options for the chosen scenario.

Shared Exploration

Share and explore each partner's ideas, understanding the reasoning behind each option without judgment.

Collaborative Solution

Together, explore creative solutions by combining aspects of both partners' ideas to form a new, mutually satisfying solution.

Final Agreement and Reflection

Reach a final agreement on the compromise solution, outlining each partner's contributions. Reflect on the collaborative process, discussing what worked well and how these skills can be applied to future scenarios.

Reflection Questions:

Describe the scenario or topic you chose for the exercise. Why did you select it, and how did you feel about tackling it together?

_____

_____

_____

Reflect on your individual brainstorming process. What ideas did you come up with, and why did you think they could be effective solutions?

_____

_____

_____

Did you encounter any challenges or limitations while brainstorming on your own?

_____

_____

_____

Share about the experience of exploring each other's ideas without judgment. How did it feel to understand your partner's perspective on the scenario?

_____

_____

_____

Did you discover any unexpected insights or common ground during this phase of the exercise?

_____

_____

_____

Discuss the process of combining aspects of both partners' ideas to form a new solution. How did you negotiate and compromise to create a mutually satisfying outcome?

_____

_____

_____

Were there any aspects of the collaborative process that you found particularly effective or challenging?

_____

_____

_____

Describe the compromise solution you reached together. How satisfied are you with the final agreement, and why?

_____

_____

_____

Reflect on the overall collaborative process. What aspects of compromise and collaboration do you feel strengthen your partnership, and how do you envision applying these skills to future scenarios?

_____

_____

_____

Chapter Seven: Criticism Instead of Constructive Feedback

When you first started dating your partner, chances are, in your eyes, they could do no wrong. Everything about them seemed perfect, and the small things that annoyed you were just their quirks, nothing more and nothing less. This was the infamous honeymoon phase of the relationship in which you are so in love that everyone around you sees it. But as time passes, you still love each other very much, and the love changes. You are in love but know your partner isn't flawless. They aren't all that perfect. You aren't either, and they might have told you as much, either in a friendly and funny way or even in a constructive way. Or, they might have told you in a way that wasn't friendly or funny, but rather in a way that hurt you – in a critical way.

When we communicate with our partners, we need to do so in a **constructive** way. We need to speak to them the same way they spoke to us. Whenever we are in the heat of an argument, this can be pretty difficult to remember. Still, it's important to remember that you should not turn to critique but should give constructive feedback. For example, if your partner is freaking out over the preparations needed for a party you are hosting, but you are much more laid-back about it than they are, instead of saying, "You always over dramatize things, and you need to control everything," you could say, "I think you like having control over certain things, but sometimes it's best to take a step back and to let other people handle it while you just relax." The way the latter is phrased is much more loving and considerate and much less likely to hurt your partner's feelings.

But what if there is something that they do wrong, and you don't know how not to make your words sound like a critique? Try focusing on how they can change to make it better. Instead of saying that something is done the *wrong* way, try to encourage them to think about how they could do it so the outcome is better. So, instead of saying, "You're always trying to control everything," try, "Why don't you take a step back here and let me handle it? I want to help you, but you need to let me take control of it." Think about how to phrase things to emphasize positive change instead of a negative starting point.

Likewise, try to ask questions. If you aren't sure what your partner's perspective is, why they are doing something this way, or their rationale, ask them. The same goes when you are on the receiving end – if your partner gives you constructive feedback and you don't understand it, ask questions! Try to deconstruct the feedback so you get more clarity on the issue. You can acknowledge their thoughts and reasoning, but you can also ask them for more information to understand better where they're coming from. Don't put up defenses – remember that they love you and want what's best for you, but they also often become the people who know us best and often better than ourselves.

If you are giving constructive feedback, try to strike a balance between input and praise. You might add a compliment, as in, "I know you like to have control over things because you need to be in control to succeed at your job, and you are very successful, but this sometimes plays against you…"

Finally, you should lead this conversation with a positive intention. Just as you should enter a conversation intending to compromise, you should also enter this type of conversation without malice. If you are annoyed or angry with them, now might not be the right time to talk about the things they do that upset you or to try and give constructive feedback! You are much more likely to end up dumping your emotions and anger on them and forgetting the other tips I've shared throughout this chapter.

This relationship is a partnership, so tell your partner how you want them to talk to you. If you wouldn't like being critiqued the way you are critiquing them, take a step back and ask yourself whether you need to talk to your partner about this right now or whether it might be best to wait a little bit and think first about how you can speak to them more positively. Hurtful communication is never good communication!

40-20-40 Relationship Exercise for Compassionate Listening and Conflict Resolution

Objective: Enhance compassionate listening and constructive conflict resolution in a relationship through the 40-20-40 process.

Steps:

Introduction and Agreement:

> Begin by introducing the 40-20-40 process, described below, to your partner. Discuss the purpose of the exercise, emphasizing the importance of compassionate listening and conflict resolution without accusatory statements. Both partners should agree to participate actively.

Individual Sharing (40% each):

> Decide on the total time for the discussion, then calculate how much each partner has to share their feelings without interruption. Each person gets 40% of the total time. For example, if you've decided on one hour for the discussion, each person will have 24 minutes. During their designated time, each person can express their thoughts, emotions, and concerns openly. The key is to avoid accusatory statements and focus on personal feelings.

Constructive Conversation (20%):

> Reserve 20% of the total time for a constructive conversation about the relationship. During this time, reflect on what was shared individually. Discuss common ground, areas of understanding, and potential solutions. The focus should be on collaboratively navigating through the concerns raised.

Active Listening and Empathy:

> Practice active listening and empathy throughout the exercise. Both partners should make a conscious effort

to listen to each other's perspectives without judgment. Validate emotions and create a safe space for open communication.

Reflect and Affirm:

Conclude the exercise with a reflective discussion. Share insights gained from the 40-20-40 process. Affirm the commitment to constructive conflict resolution and compassionate listening. Discuss any actionable steps identified during the conversation.

Reflection Questions:

How did you feel about introducing and agreeing to participate in the 40-20-40 process with your partner?

_____

_____

_____

What were your initial thoughts or expectations about the exercise?

_____

_____

_____

Reflect on your experience of sharing your feelings during your designated time. How did it feel to express yourself openly without interruption?

_____

_____

_____

Did you find it challenging to avoid accusatory statements and focus on your personal feelings? If so, what strategies did you use to overcome these challenges?

_____

_____

_____

What common ground or areas of understanding did you discover? Were you able to brainstorm potential solutions collaboratively?

_____

_____

_____

Share about your practice of active listening and empathy throughout the exercise. How did you ensure you genuinely understood your partner's perspectives without judgment?

Did you feel validated and supported by your partner during the discussion? How did you create a safe space for open communication?

Conclude the reflection by discussing insights gained from the exercise. What did you learn about your communication styles and conflict-resolution strategies?

Affirm your commitment to constructive conflict resolution and compassionate listening. Are there any specific, actionable steps or goals you identified during the conversation that you'd like to implement moving forward?

_____

_____

_____

Chapter Eight: Ignoring Your Partner's Feelings

A relationship is often called a *partnership*, as I have referred to it throughout this book. Why? Because you are *two people* working toward the same goal: having a committed, happy, and loving relationship. You are *partners* in this endeavor. You want to make things work *together*, so you agree to and commit to making it happen over the long haul. But that takes a lot of work! For a partnership to work, you have to be willing to make it work *together*. You both need to be willing to make it work, which includes listening to each other's feelings and thoughts. Unfortunately, this is something I often see being forgotten in relationships. And yet, it can make a world of difference in your relationship.

Let's start by recognizing this partnership for what it is: a core need in your relationship. Your partner is a human being who, like you, needs to be emotionally validated. Your partner wants to feel that what they share with you is accepted, heard, and respected. When they share their emotions and views, they need to feel heard and validated, like they are sharing something you relate to or are interested in hearing. Time and time again, I've seen couples who are utterly disconnected, partly because one of the partners has tried to share their feelings many times. However, the other partner still wasn't interested in hearing them out (or dismissed them altogether!). If your partner tries to tell you how they feel or tries to tell you that something you've done has made them feel unhappy, don't dismiss them; validate them first, and then discuss how they feel. Don't immediately shut them down and tell them they're wrong. Their feelings can't be wrong – that's how they feel! Instead, try to break down the reasons why they might be feeling this way. Ask them questions, but *not* to debunk their feelings. No, try to understand *why* they're feeling the way they do so you can help them stop feeling this way. This person is your partner, so don't alienate them from their feelings. Don't dismiss their feelings. Don't minimize their concerns. Don't mock how they're feeling. This is a big reason why partners become so disconnected! Over time, your partner will not feel safe sharing these things with you because you will have eroded the trust between the two of you.

It would be best if you were self-aware whenever your partner shares their feelings with you, yes, yet another buzzword, and for the same reason: It's super important. When your partner is sharing their feelings with you, please take a minute to figure out whether you are being a good partner and are listening to them or whether you are dismissing them verbally or nonverbally. Your partner shouldn't be responsible for asking you to behave appropriately or to show them more respect. You should pay attention to your behavior and ensure you are treating them well. Consider whether you might be responding to their emotions non-supportively and why that might be the case. Here's a hint: We often react negatively when we feel like we are being attacked or critiqued. And then, the human inside us jumps to the defense: Instead of listening to what our partner is saying, we defend ourselves and forget to listen to what our partner is telling us. This leads to two people who have no idea what the other is talking about and a load of miscommunication. So, before you immediately dismiss your partner's words because you feel attacked or critiqued, ask yourself if the critique is on target or whether you're being critiqued at all! Think about just listening to your partner instead of focusing on the response you're giving them or how you will protect yourself.

Your partner is just trying to tell you how they feel, not how *you* are wrong in all this. If you keep dismissing them, if you never bother listening to them or what they have to share, if you always turn the conversation around and tell them how *you* feel about what they are saying, you are not a very supportive partner. Put yourself in your partner's shoes – how do you *wish* your partner would react if you told them this? What do you wish they would say? Is this how you are responding right now? If not, think about what you can do to change your actions.

Now, let's say that you have just finished a discussion in which, despite your best efforts (and before reading this book), you turned the conversation around to yourself and your feelings and completely dismissed your partner. However, thankfully, toward the end of the conversation, you realized what you were doing and stopped dead in your tracks. What happens next? It would be best if you rebuilt trust and understanding. It would be best if you acknowledged what your actions have been like from their perspective and how they have affected your partner, and you have to outline how you will change this behavior. Show them that you know this isn't the right way to behave and that you will work on your listening skills and responses to ensure they feel more supported and validated. Then, follow through with your promises!

But what if you are the partner who's constantly being dismissed? Well, give your partner a copy of this book! In all seriousness, this is something to discuss with your partner and an opportunity for you to establish boundaries. You can start the conversation by saying, "I am not critiquing you," to lower the tension and avoid making them feel like they are on a battlefield, then continue by saying, "I would like to speak to you openly about something that's been hurting me." The goal here is to connect with them emotionally. This isn't to say that their behavior is acceptable – this is something to discuss in therapy! – but it is a short-term solution. Then, use "I" statements when sharing your emotions. Talk about how you feel, how a particular event has made you feel, how you perceive things, how you would like things to be instead, and so on. Remember the other rules in the preceding chapters, especially about not using absolute language and offering constructive feedback instead of a critique.

If you have tried everything and still struggle to get your feelings across – or understand your partner's feelings when they share them– it might be time to reach out to a couple's counselor to explore how you communicate in more detail. Sometimes, working with someone outside your marriage or partnership can be helpful because no one feels attacked – you're quite liberated to be told what to do differently, so you are much more open and receptive to feedback!

Emotional Tune-In Exercise for Couples: Enhancing Emotional Connection

Objective: Strengthening the emotional bond through structured communication.

Scheduled Reflection Sessions:

Decide on specific times for your "Reflection Sessions" with your partner. Choose a frequency that works for both of you, whether daily, weekly, or another interval. Commit to these sessions as essential for your relationship.

Experience Sharing:

Take turns sharing recent personal experiences or events that have affected your emotions. Each partner should express their feelings and briefly explain the situations or thoughts behind them.

Active Listening and Validation:

Practice active listening when your partner shares their emotions. Validate their feelings by acknowledging and understanding them without criticism or judgment.

Reciprocal Sharing:

Rotate roles in each session to ensure both partners have equal opportunities to share their emotions and experiences. Encourage openness and vulnerability in expressing feelings.

Reflective Discussion:

> Conclude each session with a reflective discussion. Share any insights gained from the reflection and discuss any patterns or changes noticed in your emotions. Explore ways to better support each other through your emotional journeys.

Reflection Questions:

How did you feel about committing to scheduled "Feelings Check-Ins" as a regular communication routine with your partner? What were your initial thoughts or reservations?

_____

_____

_____

Can you share any specific instances during the check-ins where you felt particularly connected or understood by your partner? How did these moments impact your overall perception of the exercise?

_____

_____

_____

Reflecting on your experience with the emotion wheel, how did it feel to select emotions that best represented your current feelings? Were there any emotions that surprised you or that you found challenging to articulate?

_____

_____

_____

Can you describe a situation where the emotion wheel helped facilitate a deeper understanding or conversation about your emotions with your partner? How did this contribute to your emotional connection?

_____

_____

_____

When practicing active listening during the sharing process, how did it feel to receive validation and understanding from your partner without judgment? Were there any specific moments that stood out to you?

_____

_____

_____

In what ways did your partner's responses during the exercise impact your feelings and emotional well-being? How did you feel supported or understood through their reactions?

_____

_____

_____

Reflecting on the importance of rotating roles in each session, can you share an instance where you felt particularly empowered or vulnerable when expressing your emotions? How did your partner respond, and how did it affect your emotional connection?

_____

_____

_____

How did you and your partner navigate moments of discomfort or hesitation when sharing emotions during the exercise? What strategies did you find helpful in fostering openness and vulnerability?

_____

_____

_____

As you reflect on the insights gained from the feelings check-in, are there any recurring patterns or themes in your emotional experiences that you'd like to explore further with your partner? How do you envision addressing these together?

_____

_____

_____

What specific actions or strategies can you implement to strengthen your emotional connection and support each other in navigating complex emotions? How do you plan to incorporate these into your relationship routine?

_____

_____

_____

Chapter Nine: Assuming Instead of Asking

I can't tell you how often I've had clients in my office who realize midway through the conversation that they had gotten something entirely wrong – then they say to their partner, "Why wouldn't you just ask me?" Sometimes, we hastily conclude without pausing to consider the reasons behind them. Our partner's actions, words, or expressions can trigger this tendency. Instead of listening to or inquiring about their thoughts and feelings, we rely on our assumptions to interpret the situation. Consequently, we might experience emotions like frustration or annoyance, rooted not in our beliefs but in our daily lives; failing to validate these assumptions with evidence in our relationships can lead to unnecessary conflicts that could easily be prevented.

One of the most common types of assumptions I see in my office is one partner assuming that the other one understands their point of view. I'll have two people sitting before me talking about a specific topic. Then, midway through the conversation, one or the other will have an epiphany – they had no idea that they felt a certain way or had a specific opinion. These misunderstandings emerge entirely out of assumptions, some of which could have been overcome by a bit of communication. The bottom line: When you are not sure, ask!

Do not assume that your partner understands or knows your point of view. If you have shared it with them and aren't sure whether they understand, ask them if they do. Of course, it's also their responsibility to check with *you*, as it's not only *your* responsibility to double-check and ask. However, this is a two-way street! Do not assume you understand each other's points of view, even if you've talked about it briefly. If you aren't 100% sure, it's always better to ask rather than to realize later that you both have been going off assumptions that are far from correct!

Avoiding assumptions goes beyond asking questions when you don't understand something. It's also making sure you are clear in your communication and do not assume that the other person knows something, such as how you are feeling, what you want, etc., without you telling them. So, if you miss your partner, call them, text them, just *tell* them. You can't be angry or annoyed that they aren't fulfilling your needs if you don't tell them what you need. Tell them if you need them to talk to you more or to show more love and affection because you currently don't feel like you are getting enough! The same applies if you want to meet up with them – invite them to lunch. Don't wait for an invite! You shouldn't wait for your partner to make a move, then assume they don't care if they don't make the right one. Ask them out and show that *you* care. Then, if you feel like you are the only one ever doing the inviting, that's a conversation you can have.

Communication and avoiding assumptions are also things you can work toward by making sure you are understood. In other words, you need to be willing to explain yourself. If you want your partner to understand where you are coming from or what you are feeling, you can't shut them out, give them the cold shoulder, or worse, give them the silent treatment. If that's the case, you force them to run on assumptions. Once you've talked to your partner, they can ask clarifying questions, and you can both take this opportunity to talk about what you like or dislike, what you want or do not want, what you feel needs to change, and so on.

The more you assume in your relationship, the higher the chances of one of you misunderstanding something, making decisions, or saying something based on that assumption, and hence, of conflicts arising. Why not avoid this dynamic in the first place by simply talking and being open? Become more accustomed to asking for clarification if you don't understand something, and don't assume you know everything. The same goes for your partner – if they constantly say something that sounds like an assumption and it's driving you crazy, tell them! Don't just let it happen or let it slide. You need to speak up and say it immediately – don't assume, ask! I promise you, it's likely to help you avoid most of the conflicts you're experiencing with your partner.

Prediction Method Exercise for Couples: Enhancing Understanding and Communication

Objective: Improve communication and understanding by exploring predictions of each other's reactions in various situations.

Introduction to the Prediction Method:

Begin by introducing the Prediction Method below to your partner. Explain that the exercise aims to explore and understand each person's potential reactions in different situations, promoting open communication and preventing assumptions.

Situation Identification:

Together, identify several different situations that may arise in your relationship. These can include everyday scenarios, such as who will wash the dishes and potential challenges, such as an interstate relocation. Ensure the situations cover a range of emotions and experiences.

Individual Predictions:

Individually, jot down your predictions on how your partner would react to each identified situation. Focus on being honest and considerate in your predictions. This step encourages self-reflection and awareness of assumptions.

Sharing Predictions:

Exchange your predictions with your partner. Create a safe and non-judgmental space to discuss each other's assumptions. Take turns sharing your predictions and the reasoning behind them. Encourage open dialogue to clarify any potential misunderstandings.

Response and Discussion:

Allow your partner to respond to your assumptions. Share how accurate or inaccurate the predictions were. Engage in a constructive discussion about potential differences in perception and explore ways to align expectations in various situations.

Reflection Questions:

How did you feel when introduced to the Prediction Method? What were your initial thoughts or concerns about exploring predictions of each other's reactions?

_____

_____

_____

Can you share a moment during the introduction where you and your partner felt particularly aligned or understood the purpose of the exercise? How did this impact your approach to identifying situations?

_____

_____

_____

Reflecting on identifying different situations, were there any scenarios that you found particularly challenging or enlightening to discuss? Why?

_____

_____

_____

Can you describe a situation that you both agreed upon easily? How did this agreement influence your understanding of each other's potential reactions?

_____

_____

_____

When making your predictions, what factors did you consider in imagining your partner's reactions? Were there any assumptions you caught yourself making during this process?

_____

_____

_____

Can you recall a prediction you made that surprised you after discussing it with your partner? How did this revelation impact your perception of their potential reactions?

_____

_____

_____

How did it feel to exchange predictions with your partner? Were there any predictions that sparked interesting discussions or insights into each other's perspectives?

_____

_____

_____

Can you share a moment during the prediction sharing where you felt particularly connected or understood by your partner? How did their response contribute to your sense of mutual understanding?

_____

_____

_____

Reflecting on your partner's responses to your predictions, were there any surprises or misunderstandings that emerged? How did you navigate these differences in perception?

_____

_____

_____

Can you discuss any adjustments or insights gained from the discussion that may help align expectations and improve communication in future situations?

_____

_____

_____

Chapter Ten:
Escalating Conflicts

We've reached a pivotal point in our discussion about relationships—the challenge of escalating conflicts. Throughout this book, we've explored various ways relationships can hit rough patches, often due to communication breakdowns. Misunderstandings, assumptions, blaming each other, and dredging up past issues are common pitfalls that can lead to conflicts.

But here's another critical factor we must delve into the tendency to let conflicts escalate because of a lack of emotional regulation. Picture it like this: emotions are like a storm brewing. You can sense it in the air—the tension, the change in tone, voices getting louder, and responses becoming sharper. It's like a conversation turning into a full-blown argument out of nowhere. This often happens when we struggle to step back and take a breather or lack control over our emotional reactions.

So, what can you do to avoid this? When you feel a conversation is about to turn into a conflict, don't ignore your annoyance or frustration. Instead, take a step back. Suggest to your partner that you both take a break before things get out of hand.

Facing difficulty in taking a step back during conflicts is entirely understandable, particularly if managing your emotions feels like a bit of a challenge; you might lack emotional regulation skills. Simply put, emotional regulation involves recognizing and understanding your feelings and how you express them. You might grapple with a lack of emotional regulation if you find yourself quickly overwhelmed by emotions or struggling to rein in those big emotional outbursts.

In such instances, seeking therapy could be a beneficial avenue to cultivate these crucial skills. Therapy provides a supportive environment to explore and develop effective emotional regulation strategies. However, beyond seeking professional help, there are practical steps you can take on your own.

When you're in a heated argument with your partner, consider giving yourself the gift of space. Take a breather to allow emotions to settle before diving back into the discussion. Remind yourself that the person in front of you is someone you care deeply about, and you certainly don't want to say things in the heat of the moment that you might later regret.

It's worth acknowledging that our inclination toward conflict is sometimes profoundly rooted in our past experiences. For instance, if you grew up in an environment marked by frequent conflicts, engaging in arguments might feel oddly familiar and, paradoxically, even comforting. However, it's crucial to recognize that for your partner, constant conflict can be draining and detrimental to the relationship.

Breaking free from this pattern involves a conscious effort to change your approach. Recognize when you're on the brink of escalating a conflict and challenge yourself to take a step back.

This shift not only benefits you but also alleviates the burden on your partner and the relationship as a whole.

In essence, it's about finding healthier ways to navigate disagreements and ensuring that conflicts don't become the default mode of interaction. By incorporating these intentional breaks and actively working on your emotional regulation, you pave the way for a more harmonious and resilient relationship.

Five-Minute Emotional Regulation Exercise for Couples: Cultivating Mindful Connection

Objective: Enhance emotional regulation skills and foster mindfulness together.

Joint Mindful Breathing:

Share a five-minute mindful breathing exercise. Inhale deeply for four seconds, hold for four, exhale for four, and pause for four. Focus on synchronized breath to ground yourselves in the present.

Safe Word Establishment:

Choose a "safe word" together as a signal for emotional regulation. Both partners commit to a joint timeout for mindful individual activities when used.

Individual Mindfulness Break:

During the timeout, engage in a brief individual mindfulness activity, like deep breathing or a short meditation, to regain emotional balance.

Emotion Regulation Journal:

> Keep a shared emotion regulation journal. Jot down emotions and triggers during tense moments, reflecting on patterns and identifying strategies for future emotional balance.

Mindful Communication Pause:

> Resume conversations mindfully. Use "I" statements, practice active listening, and pause with the safe word if emotions escalate. Conclude with a shared mindfulness activity for added connection.

Reflection Questions:

How did you feel during the five-minute mindful breathing exercise with your partner? Did you notice any changes in your state of mind or level of relaxation afterward?

_____

_____

_____

Can you share any insights or observations you had while focusing on synchronized breath with your partner? How did this experience contribute to your sense of connection?

_____

_____

_____

What prompted your choice of the "safe word" together? How do you envision using it to signal the need for emotional regulation during discussions or tense moments?

_____

_____

_____

Reflecting on the idea of taking a joint timeout for mindful individual activities, how do you think this practice will impact your ability to regulate emotions and maintain healthy communication?

_____

_____

_____

How did you find engaging in a brief individual mindfulness activity during the timeout? Did it help you regain emotional balance, and if so, in what ways?

_____

_____

_____

Can you describe any specific mindfulness techniques or activities that resonated with you during the individual break? How do you plan to incorporate these into your routine?

_____

_____

_____

What emotions or triggers did you jot down in the shared emotion regulation journal? Were there any patterns or recurring themes that emerged from your reflections?

_____

_____

_____

How do you envision using the emotion regulation journal to identify strategies for future emotional balance? What steps do you plan to take based on your observations?

_____

_____

_____

How did practicing mindful communication, including using "I" statements and active listening, impact your interactions with your partner? Did you find it challenging to pause with the safe word when emotions escalated?

_____

_____

_____

Reflecting on the shared mindfulness activity after conversations, how did this contribute to your sense of connection and understanding with your partner? What aspects of the activity resonated with you the most?

_____

_____

_____

Made in United States
Troutdale, OR
09/19/2024